SECRET
SCIENCE

D1119601

SECRET SCIENCE

25 Science Experiments Your Teacher Doesn't Know About

STEVE SPANGLER

SILVERLEAF
PRESS

Silverleaf Press are available exclusively
through Independent Publishers Group.

For details write or telephone
Independent Publishers Group, 814 North Franklin St.
Chicago, IL 60610, (312) 337-0747

Silverleaf Press
8160 South Highland Drive
Sandy, Utah 84093

ISBN-10: 1-933317-75-2
ISBN-13: 978-1-933317-75-5

Contents

The Science of Secrets

This book is filled with secrets, and secrets are a funny thing. Secrets come in all shapes and sizes. Everyone wants to know secrets, but you're not supposed to tell anyone secrets… or they won't be secrets any more. In simplest terms, a secret is something that you don't know, and once you learn that *something*, it's no longer a secret. Let's face it, there's just something fun about knowing a secret, but sometimes it's even more fun to share a secret.

Now you know my inspiration for writing this book. I'm not a good keeper of secrets. Maybe that's the definition of a great teacher – a person who loves to share secrets of learning.

SECRET #179:

Don't Try This at Home…. Try It at a Friend's Home!

Let's cut to the chase and be honest… science experiments have changed over the years. Okay, maybe the experiment has not changed but they way it's packaged has. All of today's science experiments come with a warning that reads, **"Do Not Try This at Home!"** Even the simplest of experiments come with this warning. We live in a day and age where everyone feels the need to share the warning… **"Do Not Try This at Home!"**

Where should you try it if not at home? I pondered about this for the longest time. You could try it at school unless it was your teacher who warned you not to try it at home. And then it came to me….. Instead of messing up your *own* home, try messing up your *friend's* home. Now the warning reads as follows…

Don't Try This at Home… Try It at a Friend's Home!

I added the discovery to my list of secrets and it became #179.

That's why the warning, "Do Not Try This at Home!", has been banned from this book. Not only *should* you try it at home but once you've mastered the activity, you should try it in *everyone's* home. You'll soon discover that almost any kitchen can be turned into a science lab, and your audiences will be amazed by your newly discovered talents. Don't be surprised if you hear people spontaneously erupt into a chorus of *ooohs & ahhhs!*

SECRET #1:

Not All Science Experiments Work

I can remember as a kid playing (I mean *experimenting*) in our garage and the basement for hours each day. It seems like I was always tinkering with something. But it wasn't blind ambition – I was on a quest to uncover the secrets of the universe. My only instruction manual was a dusty, old science book filled with experiments that promised to make something fizz, smoke, erupt, pop, change color or possibly catch on fire. It was an experimenter's dream come true… and I was hooked.

But I soon learned my first science secret – not all science experiments go as planned. Even though I gathered all the right stuff and followed the directions to the letter, the experiment didn't work – and that's part of the fun of learning. I soon learned that it really didn't matter if the experiment worked or not. The real fun was in the process of doing science. As the great science teacher, Irwin Talsenick, once told me, "Science is a verb."

The pages that follow contain some of my all-time favorite science experiments and hands-on science activities. Yes, each activity has a cool "wow" factor, and you'll amaze your friends with your newly acquired skills, but there's more. At the end of each activity, you'll learn the real science behind all of the "gee-whiz". You'll learn not only the how but the why. And then something strange will happen – you'll start to ask your own questions and create your own experiments. Don't be surprised if you a little voice in your head starts to ask things like, "What would happen if I changed this or tried that?" Curiosity will get the better of you and you'll find yourself doing the experiment again and again with your own changes and ideas.

What happens next is best part... out of the clear blue you'll make a new discovery and uncover your own science secret. You'll feel your heart start to speed up and your mind race with new ideas. You've made a discovery and that's an amazing feeling.

Good luck keeping it a secret.

A Few Science Secrets for Parents

Science is not as mysterious as we are often led to believe. Sometimes just the mention of science conjures up visions of a darkened laboratory bursting at the seams with bubbling potions, beakers of colored liquids, and, of course, there's always a mad scientist. But that's not science.

In reality, science is all about wondering, exploring, and discovery. When we observe the characteristics of something and inquire about its nature, that's science. When we wonder why the sky is blue or how the clouds are formed or why lightning strikes, we're doing science. Inquiry is at the heart of science, yet it's the skill that our children are lacking the most.

You don't need to have a degree in chemistry to help your children become better science thinkers. As parents, we should model our own curiosity by making observations about the world around us, asking questions, and trying to explain why things are the way they are. Just by being curious, observing, and asking how things work, you can pique a child's natural curiosity and create a desire to want to learn more.

Children, especially younger ones, learn science best and understand scientific ideas better if they can experiment and explore on their own. "Wondering" is an important part of any science lesson. Sometimes we forget about the wondering aspect of science and concentrate our efforts on merely teaching the facts. Science education is more than just teaching the facts. Children get turned on to science because science provides them with answers to their wonderment.

Most importantly, remember to make science **FUN**! If you are enthusiastic about exploration and scientific discovery, your enthusiasm is bound to be contagious.

My little boy, Jack, was already overflowing with a sense of wonder and a need to explore the world when he was only three years old. If Daddy was mixing up a concoction in the kitchen, rest assured that both of Jack's little hands would be in the middle of the mess. During a family picnic once, I found Jack standing at the cooler shaking up the cans of soda. I looked at him with disapproval.

"What are you doing?" I said.

"Shaking the cans," Jack replied.

"Do you know what will happen if you open that can after you shake it?" I asked.

"I can drink it?" he said, still innocent to the ways of the world.

As I walked Jack with his can of shaken soda over to an open space in the middle of the grass, it struck me that he was about to make a personal discovery that he would remember for the rest of his life. The priceless seconds that followed held surprise, bewilderment, and extreme joy for both of us. Sure, I could have just warned him that the can would explode into a fountain of soda, but he needed to discover that for himself.

The same holds true for the activities in this book. Something magical happens when you take the time to help your child explore the unknown, to make a prediction, to be right, to be wrong, or to discover something completely new. The key here is to just do it. Help your young scientist to think, reason, observe, and use their experiences to sharpen their problem solving skills.

"Daddy, can we do it again?"

May you hear that question over and over again!

Floating Ping-Pong Balls and Flying Toilet Paper

Amuse the neighbors for hours as you make objects floating in mid-air. Believe it or not, the secret to this mystery of levitation is right in front of your nose.

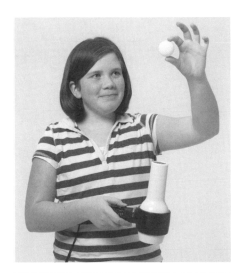

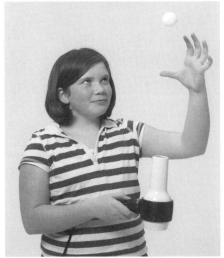

Here's What You'll Need

- Hair dryer
- Ping-pong balls
- Empty toilet paper tube
- Balloon
- Leaf blower
- Beach ball
- Roll of toilet paper

Let's Try It!

1. Set the hair dryer to cool, switch it on, and point it at the ceiling.

2. Carefully put the ping-pong ball in the stream of air. Hold the hair dryer very steady and watch as the ping-pong ball floats in the stream of air.

3. Carefully move the hairdryer from left to right and watch how the ball moves as well, staying in the stream of air.

4. Try floating other lightweight objects in the air stream at the same time! With the hair dryer on, place an inflated balloon over your levitating ping-pong ball. You might want to

place a penny in the balloon before you blow it up to give it some added weight.

Take It Further

1. Try to float two or more balls in the same air stream. How many can you float at once? How do they behave when there is more than one?

2. Need more power? Try using a leaf blower in place of the hair dryer. Now you can float larger objects like beach balls.

3. *Flying Toilet Paper!* Just hold a roll of toilet paper in the stream of air and watch the paper take off! Be sure to hold the toilet paper roll on a long stick (piece of dowel) in order for it to spin fast and unroll the paper.

4. And for the finale... Balance a ping-pong ball in the air stream. Then place your now empty toilet paper tube above it in the air. Watch it float above the ball. Then watch the ball get sucked up inside the toilet paper tube. TA-DA!! Always conclude this demo with a thanks to Bernoulli (see below if you don't get it).

Ok, What's Going On Here?

The floating ping-pong ball is a wonderful example of Bernoulli's Principle. Bernoulli, an 18th century Swiss mathematician, discovered something quite unusual about moving air. He found that the faster air flows over the surface of something, the less the air pushes on that surface (and so the lower its pressure). The air from the hair dryer flows around the outside of the ball and if you position the ball carefully, the air flows evenly around each side. Gravity pulls the ball downwards while the pressure below the ball from the moving air forces it upwards. This means that all the forces acting on the ball are balanced and the ball hovers in mid air.

You can make the ball follow the stream of air as you move the hairdryer because Bernoulli's principle says that the fast moving air around the sides of the ball is at a lower pressure than the surrounding stationary air. If the ball tries to leave the stream of air, the still, higher pressure air will push it back in—so the ball will float in the flow no matter how you move.

When you place the empty toilet paper tube into the air stream, the air is funneled into a smaller area, making air move even faster. The pressure in the tube becomes even lower than that of the air surrounding the ball, and the ball is pushed up into the tube.

Real World Application

Airplanes can fly because of Bernoulli's Principle. Air rushing over the top of airplane wings exerts less pressure than air from under the wings. So the relatively greater air pressure beneath the wings supplies the upward force, or lift, that enables airplanes to fly.

Soda Can Shake-up

Have you ever wondered why shaking a soda results in a great explosion when it's opened? Get ready to uncover some amazing soda secrets that will change your soda drinking habits.

Here's What You'll Need

- Cans of unopened soda.

Note: It's best to practice with clear liquids! Try club soda. It' not sticky. IMPORTANT: Do not use any diet soda!

Let's Try It!

1. Vigorously shake a sealed can of soda.

2. Invite a dinner guest to immediately open the can! Of course, most sane people will refuse the offer.

3. With a little science know-how, you'll be able to open the can without spilling a drop. The secret is to use your finger to snap the side of the can. This action dislodges the bubbles attached to the side of the can and they float to the top. Go ahead… snap the side of the can. Turn the can a quarter turn and snap again. Snap the side of the can at least six times before opening it.

4. Here's the truth test… open the can. Pssst! When the can is opened, the gas simply escapes and you bow to tremendous applause.

Take It Further

Once you've mastered the technique, try your newly discovered skill on different kinds of soda… but watch

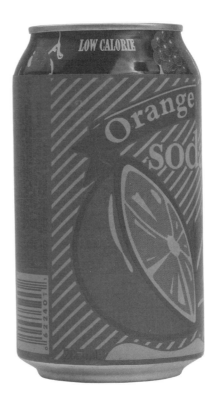

out for diet sodas. There's no guarantee that snapping the side of a can of diet soda will keep you from getting sprayed when you open the can of shaken soda. Some scientists speculate that diet sodas contain more carbon dioxide gas while others believe that there is a unique interaction that goes on between the artificial sweetener, the preservatives and the carbonated water. No one fully understands the reason other than to say you're on your own.

Ok, What's Going on Here?

Since the fizz in the soda is actually dissolved carbon dioxide gas, the goal is to keep as much of the gas in the bottle as possible. Soda fizzes when dissolved carbon dioxide gas is released in the form of bubbles. At the bottling plant, carbon dioxide molecules are forced into the soda in an amount that is greater than would ordinarily dissolve under atmospheric conditions. As soon as you open the bottle, most of the excess gas escapes into the room—that's a given! So, it's your job to find a way to keep the remaining gas in the liquid.

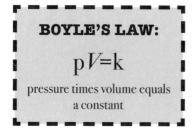

BOYLE'S LAW:

$$pV=k$$

pressure times volume equals
a constant

Shaking the unopened can of soda causes bubbles of carbon dioxide to line the inside walls of the can. When you open the can, the pressure in the can goes down and the volume of each bubble goes up. This is called "Boyle's Law." Boyle's Law states that the amount of space a gas takes up is directly related to the amount of pressure the gas is under. The can is packaged under pressure, but when you open it and the pressure goes back to normal, the quickly expanding bubbles force the liquid that rests above it out of the can.

Real Life Application

Soda pop is basically sugar (or diet sweetener), flavoring, water and preservatives. The thing that makes soda bubbly is invisible carbon dioxide gas, which is pumped into bottles at the bottling factory using lots of pressure. If you shake-up a bottle or can of soda, some of the gas comes out of solution

and the bubbles cling to the inside walls of the container (not the top). When you open the container, the bubble quickly rise to the top pushing some of the liquid out of the way. In other words, the liquid sprays everywhere!

Most people have learned to tap the top of the can before opening it. Scientifically speaking, THIS DOES NOTHING! However, tapping the side of the can knocks bubbles off the bottom and sides of the can, at which point they rise to the top. The trick is to dislodge the bubbles from the side walls and bottom of the can so they can float to the top of the can (because gas is lighter than liquid) and there will only be a small amount of liquid blocking their escape when you open the can. Remember, SNAP the SIDE instead of tapping the top.

Mentos Geyser Experiment

It's been called the "vinegar and baking soda" reaction for a new generation. Words cannot begin to describe the awesome eruption that is created from adding Mentos candies to a 2-liter bottle of soda. The eruption is enormous... and so is the learning if you consider the chemistry.

Here's What You'll Need

- A roll or box of Mentos Mints
- 2-liter bottle of diet soda (Either diet or regular soda will work for this experiment, but diet soda is less sticky when you're cleaning it up, and it will usually create a bigger blast.)

Let's Try It!

1. This activity is probably best done outside in the middle of an abandoned field or on a huge lawn.

2. Carefully open the bottle of soda. Position the bottle on the ground so that it will not tip over.

3. Unwrap the whole roll of Mentos. The goal is to drop all of the Mentos into the bottle of soda at the same time (which is trickier than it looks). One method for doing this is to roll a piece of paper into a tube just big enough to hold the loose Mentos. You'll want to be able to position the tube directly over the mouth of the bottle so that all of the candies drop into the bottle at the same time.

4. Don't drop them into the bottle just yet! Warn the spectators to stand back. Okay, you're going to drop all of the Mentos into the bottle at the same time and then get truckin' (move out of the way . . . so long . . . bye-bye . . . hasta la vista!)

5. It's just like fireworks on the 4th of July. The spectators erupt, of course, in a chorus of ooohs and ahhhs. Someone yells out, "Do it again!" and you do.

Take It Further

Experiment with different kinds of sodas to see which kinds or brands produce the biggest geysers. Does diet soda produce a bigger eruption than regular soda? Experiment with different kinds of candy. Try adding rock salt instead of Mentos to see what happens – sounds interesting!

Ok, What's Going on Here?

Why do Mentos turn ordinary diet soda into a geyser of fun? The answer may be a little more complicated than you might think. Let's start with the soda…

Drop a penny into a glass of clear soda and notice how bubbles immediately form on the surface of the penny. These are carbon dioxide bubbles leaving the soda they are dissolved into and attaching themselves to the penny. Now try adding salt to the soda. See how it foams up? This is because thousands of tiny bubbles are forming on the surface of each grain of salt, just like they did on the penny. This is called *nucleation* and the places that the bubbles form, whether on the sides of a can, on a penny, or around a tiny grain of salt, are called *nucleation sites*.

Why are Mentos so special

The reason why Mentos work so well is two fold — tiny pits on the surface of the candy and the weight of the candy. Each Mentos candy has thousands of tiny pits all over the surface. These tiny pits act as nucleation sites. As soon as the Mentos hit the soda, bubbles form all over the surface of the candy and then quickly rise to the surface of the liquid. Couple this with the fact that the Mentos candies are heavy and sink to the bottom of the bottle and you've got a double-whammy. When all this gas is released, it literally pushes all of the liquid up and out of the bottle on its way up in an incredible soda blast.

When you're done creating geysers, pour the remaining soda out of the bottle and take a look at the Mentos. You can actually see the nucleation sites where the soda has eaten away at the surface of the candy. No need to waste the candy… they still taste great.

Sinking Soda Surprise

Plug the drain, fill the sink with water, and take the plunge with Steve Spangler's floating science challenge.

Here's What You'll Need

- An assortment of unopened soda cans (diet, regular, brand name, generic)
- A large, deep container of water like a
  5 gallon bucket or an aquarium

Let's Try It!

1. Ask your audience the question: "Will this can of regular soda float or sink in the bucket of water?" After gathering everyone's answer, place the can of regular soda in the water and notice that it sinks to the bottom.

Note: If the can of regular soda

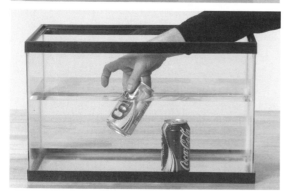

floats, you might have an air bubble trapped under the bottom of the can. Turn it on its side and it should sink.

2. Pick up a can of diet soda and pose the same question. Be sure to point out the fact that the cans are exactly the same size and shape and contain the same amount of liquid (compare the number of milliliters—probably 355 ml). Place the can of diet soda in the water. It floats! Wobble the can from side to side to show your audience that there are no bubbles trapped under the bottom. It still floats. Why?

3. Let your group experiment with different kinds of soda. Why do the diet sodas float and the regular soda cans sink, no matter the brand? It's a scientific question.

Ok, What's Going On Here?

This demonstration is an excellent way to learn about density. We are all familiar with the basic concept of sinking or floating. Objects less dense than water float, and those denser than water sink. Empty cans float, rocks sink. This is only possible because of differences in density, or mass in relation to volume.

If both diet and regular soda

cans could be placed on a double pan balance (like the one blindfolded Lady Justice carries), it would be clear that regular soda is heavier than diet soda. This demonstrates the difference between mass and volume. Mass refers to how much stuff exists within an object. If something is heavier than another object, it contains more mass. Mass is measured in grams.

Volume, on the other hand, refers to how much space an object occupies. For fluids, volume is usually measured in liters (L) or milliliters (ml). This is what we were referring to when we told you that the cans contained the same amount of liquid—233 ml. Since both cans have the same volume, the heavier can must have a greater mass. We can now conclude that the heavier can is denser than the lighter can.

The scientific secret is that diet sodas usually contain aspartame, an artificial sweetener, while regular sodas use regular sugar. Take a look at the nutritional information on the side of the cans. Notice how much sugar is in a regular soda (look under carbohydrates). Most regular sodas have about 41 grams of sugar. How much is 41 grams? Try 18 packets of sugar like the ones you might find at a restaurant! Diet soda is flavored with an artificial sweetener (like aspartame), which is 200 times sweeter than an equal amount of sugar. Therefore, only a tiny amount of aspartame is needed. Both sugar and aspartame are denser than water, which can be easily demonstrated by adding small amounts of each to a container of water (They sink!). So it is actually a matter of how much of each is used. The 41 grams or so of sugar added to a can of regular soda makes it sink. The relatively tiny amount of aspartame used in diet sodas will have a negligible effect on the mass. Still, you might wonder why diet cans of soda float. What makes liquid soda lighter than liquid water?

It is all due to the fact that there is a little bit of space, called *headspace*, above the fluid in each can of soda. This space is filled with carbon dioxide gas, which is much less dense than the soda itself. It is this space above the soda that lowers the density of diet drinks just enough to make them float. Sugared drinks also have this headspace, but the excessive amount of sugar added makes the can denser than water.

Floating Bowling Balls

We all know that certain things float in water while other things sink, but why? Do all heavy things sink? Why does a penny sink and an aircraft carrier float? Plug the drain, fill the sink with water, and take the plunge with Steve's floating science challenge.

Here's What You'll Need

- 2 or more bowling balls. The next time you're at the bowling alley, sneak an aquarium filled with water in under your coat. Too risky? Ok, just collect a few bowling balls of various weights (from 8 to 16 pounds). You might want to stop by your local bowling alley to see if the pro shop is throwing away any old bowling balls that you might be able to use for your science entertainment pleasure.

Note: Be sure that at least one weighs 10 pounds or less and at least one weighs 12 pounds or more.

- Large aquarium or bath tub filled with water

Let's Try It!

1. Fill the aquarium three quarters full with water.

2. Carefully place (do not drop!) the bowling ball in the water. Does it float or sink? Repeat this

experiment, noting the weight of each bowling ball, until every ball has taken the plunge.

3.   What did you discover? It seems that anything heavier than 12 pounds will sink, but bowling balls between 8 and 12 pounds float. Amazing!

Ok, What's Going On Here?

Hey, are you pulling my leg? NO! The bowling balls that we used in our experiment were legitimate, competition-sanctioned bowling balls. For those disbelievers, the water was real, too. We suggest using an 8 pound ball for your less dense ball since it floats fairly high but a 9 or 10 pound ball will

work just as well. Anything heavier than 12 pounds will sink.

If you've ever been bowling you know that bowling balls range from about 8 to 16 pounds. However they are all the same size! According to the official bowling rules: "The circumference of a ball shall not be more than 27.002 inches nor less than 26.704 inches, nor shall it weigh more than 16 pounds (no minimum weight)." This means that the average density of an 8-pound ball must be HALF the average density of a 16-pound ball. In general, bowling ball manufacturers vary the size, shape and material of the core of the ball to adjust the weight.

Now let's review some properties of

water. How heavy is 8 pounds? It just happens to work out that one gallon of water weighs 8 pounds. Hmmm? Well, if one gallon of water weighs 8 pounds and an 8-pound bowling ball takes up more space than a gallon of water, the ball will float!

What did Archimedes say about all of this? When an object is placed in water it will displace its weight in water. The 8 pound ball is displacing 8 pounds of water. However, the ball also takes up more volume than 8 pounds of water, so it floats. It might be less confusing to simply say the 8 pound ball is less dense than water and the 16 pound ball is denser than water.

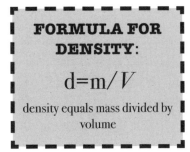

FORMULA FOR DENSITY:

$$d = m/V$$

density equals mass divided by volume

Take It Further

Don't limit your curiosity to bowling balls alone. Try to float anything. Will a bottle of ketchup float or sink? Will a rubber chicken float or sink? How about an orange? Here's something strange... an unpeeled orange floats but a peeled orange sinks. Hmmm? Any guesses? Tiny pockets of air are trapped in the orange rind that make the unpeeled orange float in water. The game is a great way for you to practice formulating a hypothesis, testing a theory, and using what you know (or don't yet know) about density to communicate the reason why an object floats or sinks, just like a real scientist!

Bubbling Lava Bottle

Learn how to make a wave bottle using oil and water and a secret ingredient that makes the whole thing fizz, bubble, and erupt.

Here's what you'll need...

- You'll need to find a clean, plastic soda bottle with a cap (16 oz. size works well)
- Vegetable oil (cheap is best)
- Food coloring
- Alka-Seltzer tablet
- Water.

Let's Try It!

1. Fill the bottle 3/4 full with vegetable oil.

2. Fill the rest of the bottle with water (almost to the top but not overflowing).

3. Add about 10 drops of food coloring. Be sure to make the water fairly dark in color. Notice that the food coloring only colors the water and not the oil. Hmmm?

4. Divide the Alka-Seltzer tablet into 8 pieces.

5. Drop one of the tiny pieces of Alka-Seltzer into the oil and water mixture. Watch what happens. When the bubblingstops, add another chunk of Alka-Seltzer. It's just like a lava lamp!

6. When you have used up all of the Alka-Seltzer and the bubbling

has completely stopped, screw on the soda bottle cap. Tip the bottle back and forth and watch the wave appear. The tiny droplets of liquid join together to make one big wave-like blob.

Ok, What's Going On Here?

First of all, you confirmed what you already knew… oil and water do not mix. The molecules of water do not like to mix with the molecules of oil. Even if you try to shake up the bottle, the oil breaks up into small little drops, but the oil doesn't really mix with the water. Also, food coloring only mixes with water. That's why it does not color the oil.

When you poured the water into the soda bottle with the oil, the water sank to the bottom and the oil floated to the top. This is the same as when oil from a ship spills in the ocean. The oil will float on top of the water. That's because water is heavier than oil. Scientists say that the water is *denser* than the oil.

Here's the surprising part. . . . The Alka-Seltzer tablet reacts with the water to make tiny bubbles of carbon dioxide gas. These bubbles attach themselves to the blobs of colored water and drag them with them to float to the surface. When the bubbles pop, the color blobs sink back to the bottom of the bottle. Now that's a burst of color!

Pop Your Top

What happens when you have a build-up of gas? Don't answer that question! The gas in question in this experiment is carbon dioxide (represented by the symbol CO_2) and the explosion is nothing short of fun. *Warning: It's impossible to do this activity just once. It is addicting and habit-forming. Proceed at your own risk!*

Here's What You'll Need

- 2 Alka-Seltzer tablets
- Film canister with a snap-on lid. Get a clear film canister if possible.
- Safety glasses
- Paper towels for clean up (you already know that this one is going to be good!)
- Watch or timer
- Notebook
- Adult helper

Let's Try It!

1. Put on your safety glasses.

2. Divide the Alka-Seltzer tablet into four equal pieces.

3. Fill the film canister 1/2 of the way full with water.

4. Get ready to time the reaction of Alka-Seltzer and water. Place one of the pieces of Alka-Seltzer tablet in the film canister. What happens?

5. Time the reaction and write the time down. How long does the chemical reaction

last? In other words, how long does the liquid keep bubbling? Why do you think the liquid stops bubbling? Empty the liquid from the film canister into the waste bucket.

6. Repeat the experiment, but this time place the lid on the container right after you drop the piece of Alka-Seltzer into the canister. Remember to start timing the reaction as soon as you drop the piece of Alka-Seltzer into the water. Oh, by the way, *stand back!* If you're lucky, the lid will pop off and fly into the air at warp speed.

7. You should have two pieces of Alka-Seltzer tablet left. Repeat the experiment using one of the pieces of Alka-Seltzer, but this time you decide on the amount of water to put in the film canister. Do you think that it will make any difference?

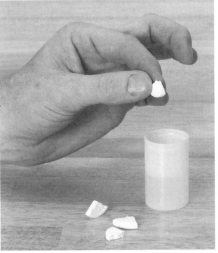

8. Use the last piece of Alka-Seltzer to make up your own experiment. What do you want to find out? How are you going to do it? What are you going to measure?

9. Go ahead and experiment!

Take It Further

If you have another Alka-Seltzer tablet, divide it into four equal pieces. This time you're going to determine if changing the

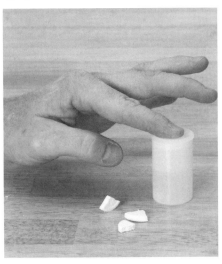

temperature of the water has any affect on the speed of the reaction. Repeat step 6 and write down your observations. You may need to experiment with several different film canisters until you find one that really pops.

Ok, What's Going On Here?

The science secret is actually hiding in the bubbles that you observed the fist time through. The Alka-Seltzer tablet reacts with the water to create carbon dioxide gas (all of those bubbles). Carbon dioxide gas builds up so much pressure inside the closed film canister that the lid pops off. This is a great example of a chemical reaction between the water and the Alka-Seltzer. You also

discovered that temperature plays an important part of the reaction as well. Warm water speeds up the reaction while colder water takes longer to build up enough pressure to pop off the lid.

Alka-Seltzer Rocket

Here's a clever variation of the classic Pop Your Top activity, but this time you launch the bottom of the film canister like a rocket! It's all about the carbon dioxide, baby!

Here's What You'll Need

- Empty paper towel roll (the cardboard tube) or a similar size plastic tube
- Film canister (Fuji brand work best)
- Duct tape
- Alka-Seltzer tablet
- Water
- Safety glasses

IMPORTANT: Safety glasses must be worn for this activity.

Let's Try It!

1. Start by sealing the end of the tube with several pieces of duct tape or use a plastic tube with one end sealed.

2. Divide the Alka-Seltzer tablet into four equal pieces.

3. Fill the film canister 1/2 of the way full with water.

Note: The next few steps have to take place very quickly or the rocket will blast off before your ready. Read through the next few steps first and make sure you understand what is going to happen before trying it.

4. Place one of the pieces of Alka-Seltzer tablet in the film

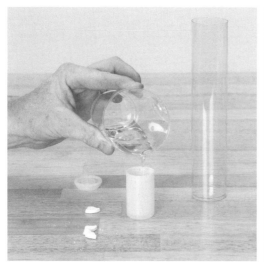
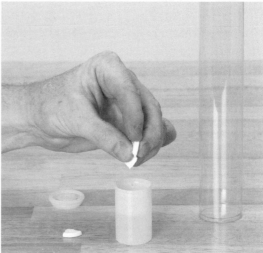

canister and quickly snap the lid on the container.

5. Turn the film canister upside down and slide it (lid first) into the tube.

6. Point the open end of the tube AWAY from yourself and others and wait for pop. Instead of the lid flying off, the bottom of the film canister shoots out of the tube and flies across the room to the cheers of the innocent bystanders.

7. Listen carefully and you'll hear people yelling, "Do it again!" What are you waiting for? Do it again!

Take It Further

Once you've mastered the technique, it's time to measure how far the film canister rocket flies across the room.

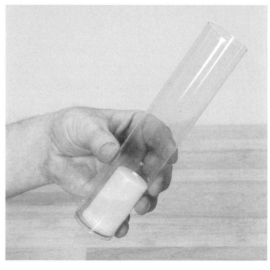

After each trial, write down the amount of water you used in the film canister, the size of the piece of Alka-Seltzer (this should not change) and the distance the film canister traveled. What amount of water mixed with a quarter piece of Alka-Seltzer tablet produced the best rocket fuel.

After you've determined the best amount of water to use, try changing the temperature of the water. How does this affect the speed of the reaction? Does warmer or colder water change the distance that the film canister travels?

If you're really creative, you can use construction paper to turn the bottom part of the film canister into a rocket. Wrap some paper around the canister, add some fins and top the whole thing off with a nose cone and you've got an Alka-Seltzer powered rocket.

Ok, What's Going On Here?

The fizzing you see when you drop an Alka-Seltzer tablet in water is the same sort of fizzing that you see when you mix baking soda and vinegar. The acid in vinegar mixes with the sodium bicarbonate (baking soda) to produce bubbles of carbon dioxide gas. If you look at the ingredients for Alka-Seltzer, you will find that it contains citric acid and sodium bicarbonate (baking soda). When you drop the tablet in water, the acid and the baking soda react to produce carbon dioxide gas, and this gas keeps building up until the pressure finally pops the top off.

We can thank Sir Isaac Newton for what happens next. When the build up of carbon dioxide gas is too great and the lid pops off, but the lid resting against the sealed bottom of the tube has nowhere to go. So all of the force of the explosion is directed against the film cannister bottom which is free to move.

Scientists know that Newton's Third Law explains why the film cannister flies across the room: *For every action there is an equal and opposite reaction.*

Floating Water

Is it really possible to fill a glass with water and turn it upside down without spilling any water? How is that possible? It doesn't sound trure, but follow these simple instructions and you'll amaze yourself!

Here's What You'll Need

- Plastic Cup
- Index card or old playing card
- Tub or sink to practice over

Let's Try It!

1. Fill the plastic cup almost to the top with water.

2. Cover the cup with an old playing card making sure that the card completely covers the mouth of the container.

3. Keep your hand on the playing card and turn the plastic cup upside down. Hold the cup over the tub just in case you accidentally spill.

4. Take your hand away and the card will stay in place. So should the water (keep your fingers crossed).

Take It Further

Repeat the experiment, but this time change the amount of water in the cup. Does it make any difference?

What about if you switch the container? Will a wider cup hold the card better or worse?

AIR PRESSURE FORMULA:

$$14.7\,a = P$$

14.7 pounds of air pressure times the
total area of the lid surface equals the
total amount of air pressure

Try the experiment using a paper
cup or plastic cup, but this time poke a
hole in the bottom of the cup. What do
you predict will happen if air is allowed
to sneak into the cup?

Ok, What's Going On Here?

The science secret is right in front of
your nose. It's the air that we breathe.
The card stays in place because the air
molecules pushing on the outside of the
cup are greater than the pressure of the
air pushing inside the cup. Air molecules
in the atmosphere are exerting pressure
on everything. Scientists know that air
molecules in the atmosphere exert 14.7
pounds of pressure per square inch of
surface at sea level.

When you turn the cup upside
down, the pressure of the air inside and
outside the cup is equal… but if you
look closely, you'll notice that just a little
amount of water leaks out between the

card and the cup. This happens because the force of gravity naturally pulls down on the water. When some of the water escapes, this causes the volume of air above the water to increase slightly. Even though the amount of air above the water stays the same, the space it occupies grows greater when the water leaks out.

Remember "Boyle's Law"? The amount of space a gas takes up is directly related to the amount of pressure the gas is under. If the amount of air (the gas) remains the same, and its volume increases, the amount of pressure must go down. When this happens, the pressure of the air pushing on the outside of the cup is greater than the pressure of the air pushing from the inside of the cup, and the card stays in place! All of this is possible because the water to created an air-tight seal between the rim of the cup and the card.

Poking a hole in the cup allows air to seep into the cup from the outside, maintaining a constant pressure. When the pressure of the air molecules both inside and outside the cup are the same, gravity takes over, the card falls, and the water spills. Isn't science amazing!

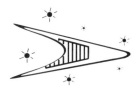

Mysterious Water Suspension

Fill the glass jar with water and cover it with a card. As you turn the whole thing upside down, the audience can hardly contain themselves. The room quiets down as you precariously position the inverted jar and card a few feet above someone's head. Just as they thought, no water spills out because the card magically sticks to the mouth of the upside down jar. But wait... there's more.

Here's What You'll Need

- Mason jar (pint size) with twist-on lid
- Plastic screen material
- Scissors
- Index cards

Let's Try It!

1. Place the plastic screen material over the opening of the jar and screw on the lid (sealing ban). Remove the lid and use scissors to cut around the indentation. What you're left with is the screen insert that fits perfectly into the top of the sealing band.

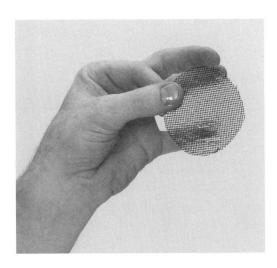

2. Place the screen over the opening of the jar and twist on the lid. Make sure that you do not accidentally show your audience the secret screen.

3. When you're ready to perform the trick, fill the jar with water by simply pouring water through the screen.

4. Cover the opening with the index card. Hold the card in place as you turn the card and the jar upside down.

5. Carefully remove the card from the opening and the water mysteriously stays in the jar!

6. Replace the card, turn the whole thing over.

7. Remove the card and pour out the water. That's amazing!

Take It Further

Experiment with different screens, some with fine mesh and some with coarse mesh, to observe how surface tension and air pressure work together to accomplish the feat. For different screens, try materials such as cloth, plastic mesh from produce bags, etc.

See what happens when different sizes and shapes of bottles are used.

Ok, What's Going On Here?

You learned that the card stays on because the pressure of the air molecules pushing up on the card is greater than the weight of the water pushing down. But how does the water stay in the jar when the card is removed? The answer? Surface Tension!

The surface of a liquid behaves as if it has a thin membrane stretched over it. A force called cohesion, which is the attraction of molecules that are the same to each other, causes this effect. The surface tension "membrane" is always trying to contract, which explains why falling droplets of water are spherical or ball shaped. The water stays in the jar even though the card is removed because the molecules of water are joined together to form a thin membrane between each opening in the screen. Be careful not to giggle the jar or touch the screen because you'll break the surface tension and surprise everyone with a gush of water!

Balancing Nails

The object of the challenge is to balance all of the nails on the head of a single nail. All of the nails have to be balanced at the same time and cannot touch anything but the top of the nail that is stuck in the base. Are you up to the challenge?

Here's What You'll Need

- Block of wood (4 inches square and about 1/2 an inch thick)
- 12 identical nails with heads (nails should be 10-penny size or larger)

Let's Try It!

1. Hammer one of the nails into the center of the block of wood.

   Note: It's a good idea to measure and pre-drill the hole to avoid splitting the wooden block.

2. Place the wood block flat on a desk or table. To win the challenge, none of the 11 nails may touch the wood block, the desk or table, or anything else that might help hold them up. No additional equipment other than the wood block and the nails may be used.

3. Need help? The trick to balancing the nails has

to do with their "center of gravity" or balancing point. Lay one nail on a flat surface and place other nails across this nail, head to head as shown in the photograph. Finally, place

another nail on top of this assembly, head to tail with the second nail.

4. Carefully pick up the assembly and balance it on the upright nail. Voila!

Take It Further

Slowly remove one nail at a time. How many nails could you remove before the system collapsed? Which nails were necessary for the system to remain in balance?

Ok, What's Going On Here?

Gravity pulls any object down as if all of its weight were concentrated at one point. That point is called the "center of gravity." Objects fall over when their center of gravity is not supported. For symmetrical objects like a ball or a meter stick, the center of gravity is exactly in the middle of the object. For objects that are not symmetrical like a baseball bat, the center of gravity is closer to the heavier end.

The stability of the nails depends on their center of gravity being right at or directly below the point where they rest on the bottom nail. Add too many nails to the left or right and they become unstable and fall off.

The Baby Diaper Secret

If you've ever changed a diaper and noticed what looked like tiny crystals on the baby's skin, you've uncovered the secret of super-absorbent, disposable diapers. Those tiny crystals actually come from the lining of the diaper and are made out of a safe, non-toxic polymer that absorbs moisture away from the baby's skin.

Here's What You'll Need

- Disposable diapers (several brands)
- Zipper-lock bag
- Scissors
- Newspaper
- Water

Let's Try It!

1. Place a new (unused is your first choice) diaper on the piece of newspaper. Carefully cut through the inside lining and remove all the cotton-like material. Put all the stuffing material into a clean, zipper-lock bag.

2. Scoop up any of the polymer powder that may have spilled onto the paper and pour it into the bag with the stuffing. Blow a little air into the bag to make it puff up like a pillow, then seal the bag.

3. Shake the bag for a few minutes to remove the powdery polymer from the stuffing. Notice how much (or how little) powder falls to the bottom of the bag.

4. Carefully cut off the corner of the zip-lock bag so that you have a little pocket of the polymer.

5. Pour the polymer into a plastic cup and fill the cup with water. Mix it with your finger until the mixture starts to thicken.

6. Observe the gel that the polymer and water have created. Turn the cup upside-down and see how it has entirely solidified. Take it out and play with it. Amazing stuff!

Take It Further

Gather the pieces of gel into a cup and smoosh it down with your fingers. Add a teaspoon of salt, stir it with a spoon, and watch what happens. Salt messes up the gel's water-holding abilities! When you're finished, pour the salt water goo down the drain.

Ok, What's Going On Here?

The secret, water-absorbing chemical in a diaper is a super-absorbent polymer called sodium polyacrylate. A polymer is simply a long chain of repeating molecules. If the prefix "poly" means many, then a polymer is a large molecule made up of many smaller units, called *monomers*, which are joined together. Some polymers are made up of millions of monomers.

Superabsorbent polymers expand tremendously when they come in contact with water because water molecules are drawn into and held by the molecules of the polymer. They act

like giant sponges. Some can soak up as much as 800 times their weight in water!

The cotton-like fibers you removed from the diaper are there to spread out both the polymer and the, uh, "water" so that baby doesn't have to sit on a gooshy lump of water-filled gel. It's easy to see that even a little bit of powder will hold a huge quantity of liquid, but it does have its limits. At some point, baby will certainly let you know when the gel is full and it's time for new undies!

Real World Application

In spite of their usefulness, these diapers can be a problem. If you've ever observed a baby in diapers splashing in a wading pool, you know that even one diaper can absorb lots and lots of water! Most public pools won't allow them to be worn in the water because huge globs of gooey gel can leak out and make a mess of the filter system. Also, some folks used to throw diapers away by flushing them down the toilet—not a good idea unless you're a plumber.

But for the most part, these diapers are a great invention and make dry, happy babies!

The Quick-Pour Soda Bottle Race

Race to see who can empty a 2-liter soda bottle full of water first. With a special twist of the hand, you will be able to empty the water in the soda bottle in just a few seconds.

Here's What You'll Need

- Plastic soda bottle (1 or 2 liter size)
- Pitcher of water
- Marker, any color
- Stopwatch or watch with a second hand to record your times

Let's Try It!

1. Fill the soda bottle to the top with water and mark with a marker where the top of the water reaches.

2. Without squeezing the sides of the bottle, turn it over and time how long it takes to empty all of the water. To get a more scientific result, you might want to repeat this several times and average the results.

Note: Be sure to fill the bottle up to the mark you madeach time. That way you'll be sure to use the same amount of water for each trial.

3. Keep a table of the trials and label this the "Glug-Glug

Method."

4. Fill the bottle to the top with the same amount of water as you did before. However, when

you turn it over this time, move the bottle in a tight, clockwise or counter-clockwise circular motion as the water pours out.

5. Keep moving the bottle like this until you see the formation of what looks like a tornado in the bottle! The water begins to swirl, a vortex forms, and water flows out of the bottle very quickly.

6. Time this method as before and mark down your results in the table, only call it the "Vortex Method." Which method works faster?

Take It Further

See if you can figure out new methods for getting the water out quickly. Try shaking the bottle up and down. Time your trials and record them. Get another bottle and challenge your friends to a race. Until they learn the secret, you will win every time.

Ok, What's Going On Here?

Swirling the water in the bottle while pouring it out causes the formation of a *vortex*. A vortex is a liquid whirling around a common center. It looks like a tornado in the bottle. The formation of the vortex makes it easier for air to come into the bottle and allows the water to pour out faster. If you look carefully, you will be able to see the hole in the middle of the vortex that allows the air to come up inside the bottle. If you do not swirl the water but just allow it to flow out on its own, then the air and water have to take turns passing through the mouth of the bottle.

Real World Application

The plural of vortex is *vortices*. Vortices are found in nature in fast flowing rivers, where the water has to go around a corner or around a large rock. In pools below a waterfall, we can also find vortices caused by strong currents of water. The pressure in the center of a vortex is lower than its surrounding outer area so it pulls everything around it into the center and down. Swimming near a waterfall can be quite dangerous. Experts suggest that if you were to get caught in a vortex, the best thing to do to get out of it would be to go with the flow all the way down to the bottom of the vortex and come up to the surface at another spot. You should never struggle to swim up to the surface against a vortex as this will actually keep you under the water longer. Good to know!

Straw Through Potato

Sometimes you have to stop and ask yourself, "Who comes up with this stuff?" No one ever uses a straw to eat a potato, but science nerds seem to like to find ways to poke straws through potatoes. There must be a deeper meaning... and there is!

Here's What You'll Need

- 2 or more stiff straws
- Big, raw potato
- Paper towels to clean up afterwards

Let's Try It!

1. The challenge is quite simple: Stab the straw through the potato without bending or breaking the straw. Most of your guests will think it can't be done, but you, of course, know better.

2. As you hold the potato, keep your fingers on the front and thumb on the back and not on the top and bottom—you don't want to stab yourself! Grab the

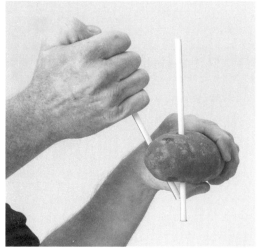

straw with your writing hand and (this is the secret) cap the top end with your thumb.

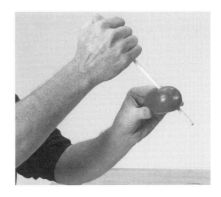

3. Hold on firmly to both the straw and the potato and with a quick, sharp stab, drive the straw into and partway out of the narrow end of the spud (not the fatter, middle part). You're so cool!

4. Your audience will be impressed and want to try it. Great! Tell them to hold the spud the way you did so they don't stab a finger or thumb with the straw. They may not know the secret, so don't give it away just yet. You may need more stiff straws for them too.

Take It Further

You know exactly where to go next. Open the refrigerator and search for your favorite fruits and vegetables that seem to be best suited for a straw attack.

Ok, What's Going On Here?

The secret is inside the straw: it's air! Placing your thumb over the end of the straw traps the air inside. When you trap the air inside the straw, the air molecules compress and give the straw strength, which in turn keeps the sides from bending as you jam the straw through the potato. The trapped, compressed air makes the straw strong enough to cut through the skin, pass through the potato, and out the other side. Without your thumb covering the hole, the air is simply pushed out of the

straw and the straw crumples and breaks as it hits the hard potato surface.

Make sure to keep your fingers out of the way. After you stab the straw, take a look at the end that passed through the potato. There's a plug-o'-spud inside the straw. If you should have a finger or thumb or hand in the way of the straw as it collides with the potato, then there will be a plug-o'-you in the straw too. Ouch!

The Leak-Proof Bag

Who would have ever thought that a plastic bag, some water, and a few pencils would frighten the thunder out of Mom? Learn how to poke a hole in a plastic bag filled with water and reseal it like magic. The secret has to do with a better understanding of the chemistry of polymers.

Here's What You'll Need

- 5 pencils with round edges
- Resealable plastic bag
- Water
- A few paper towels

Let's Try It!

1. Start by sharpening the pencils. Make sure the tips of the pencils are sharpened to a point.

2. Fill the bag 1/2 full with water and then seal the bag closed.

Pose this question to your dinner guests, "What would happen if I tried to push one of these pencils through the bag of water? Will

the water leak out and make a giant mess?" Yes . . . unless you know the scientific secret.

3.   Here comes the scary part. Hold the pencil in one hand and the top of the bag in the other hand. Believe it or not, you can push the pencil right through one side of the bag and half way out the other side without spilling a drop. The bag magically seals itself around the pencil. Sounds impossible? Try it—over the sink for the first time!

Note: Be careful not to push the pencils all the way through the holes or your "spear-it" experiment will turn into a big "clean-up-the-water" activity.

4.   Continue to rekindle your "spear-it" for science by jabbing the remaining pencils through the bag.

5. When you are finished, remove the pencils while holding the bag over the sink. Throw away the bag and dry the pencils.

Take It Further

Try experimenting with bags of different thickness. The thicker the bag, the harder it is to get the pencil to pass through. Experiment with different sizes and shapes of pencils. You might discover that a pencil without round edges causes the bag to leak. Why?

Ok, What's Going On Here?

The plastic bag is made out of long

$$\cdots \diagdown C \diagup \overset{\overset{\textstyle H_2}{C}}{} \diagdown C \diagup \cdots$$

$$H_2 \qquad\qquad H_2$$

A common polymer like Polyethene is made up of thousands of ethylene molecules bonded together like this.

chains of molecules called polymers. This gives the bag its stretchy properties. The sharpened pencils slip between the molecule strands without tearing the entire bag. Believe it or not, the long chains of molecules seal back around the pencil to prevent leaks.

Diving Ketchup

Cause a packet of ketchup to rise and fall on command in a bottle of water. People will think that you have the ability to move objects with your mind! Telekinesis? No, just cool science!

Here's What You'll Need

- Clear plastic soda bottle with cap
- Ketchup packet that floats
- Water

Let's Try It!

1. First, you'll need to perform a "float or sink" test to see how the ketchup packet works. Not all packets will float and you need one that will float for this experiment. Fill a glass with water and drop the packet into it. If it floats, great! If it sinks to the bottom, no sweat. This shows that atmospheric pressure in the packet is pressing hard enough on the air bubble inside the packet to sink it. If this happens, you get to make more trips to your favorite fast food restaurant to find a ketchup packet that just barely floats!

2. Scrunch the packet in half lengthwise and carefully push it into the soda bottle.

3. Fill the bottle full to the brim with

water and screw on the cap.

4. Squeeze the sides of the bottle to make the packet sink. Let go and it rises. It's not magic, it's science.

Take It Further

What other condiments can you cause to float and sink on command? It's time to start collecting mustard, mayonnaise, hot sauce, soy sauce and any other packet that might fit the floating

requirement. Your friends are going to think that you're crazy… but you're learning the fine art of experimentation.

Ok, What's Going On Here?

The packet floats because an air bubble gets trapped inside the packet when it's sealed at the factory. If the packet sinks when you test-float it, then the air bubble is too small to make it float. That's the easy part.

As you squeeze the bottle and push the water against the floating packet, you compress the air bubble into a smaller space. This happens because gases are more "squishable" than liquids, so the air compresses before the water does. When you decrease the volume (making the bubble of air smaller), you increase the total density of the packet and it sinks! When you release the pressure on the bottle, the compressed air expands inside the packet and the diving ketchup floats to the top of the bottle.

Do Not Open Bottle

If it says DO NOT OPEN, someone will want to open it. Guaranteed. It's fun to EXPERIENCE science!

Here's What You'll Need

- Clear plastic soda bottle (2-liter with cap)
- Deep sink or large pan
- Permanent marker, any color
- Sharp push pin
- An adult assistant

Let's Try It!

1. Clean and dry the 2-liter bottle and remove the label.

2. Use the permanent marker to write "DO NOT OPEN!" in fat letters on the bottom half of the bottle.

3. *Have your adult assistant do this step*: Use a sharp pushpin and carefully poke tiny holes through the bottle inside the color of all of the letters.

4. Place the bottle in a deep sink or pan and fill it with water. This is the tricky part. Water will leak out of the holes as you're filling the bottle. Keep the water running as you screw on the cap. Once the cap is in place, the water should stop leaking out of the holes!

5. Carefully set the bottle on the kitchen counter (word-side out) where someone can see it as they pass by.

   Note: Be careful not to squeeze the bottle or it will start leaking before you're ready.

6. Stay close enough to watch what happens. Eventually, someone is bound to ask about the bottle. Play dumb with, "I dunno" when they ask about it. Let them unscrew the cap and you'll witness science in action!

Take It Further

Experiment by poking holes in different parts of the bottle. Does the size of the hole matter? Does it matter if you poke through the marker or just through the unmarked side of the bottle? What if you poke the bottom instead of the sides?

Ok, What's Going On Here?

Let's start by examining an empty soda bottle. Is the bottle really empty? No. The bottle is filled with air (gotcha!). When you pour water into the bottle, the invisible molecules of air that once occupied the bottle come rushing out of the top. You don't notice this because molecules of air are invisible (duh!). When you turn a bottle filled with water

upside down, the water pours out (thanks to gravity) and air rushes into the bottle. Think of it as an even exchange of water for air.

You might think that poking a tiny hole in the side of a bottle would cause it to leak, and it does if air molecules can sneak into the bottle. When the lid is on the soda bottle, air pressure can't get into the bottle to push on the surface of the water. The tiny holes in the side of the bottle are not big enough for the air to sneak in. Believe it or not, the water molecules work together to form a kind of skin to seal the holes—it's called *surface tension*. When the lid is uncapped, air sneaks in through the top of the bottle and pushes down on the water (along with the force of gravity) and the water squirts through the holes in the bottom of the bottle. You know you're doing something right whenever people scream at your science experiments!

The Spinning Penny

It's an amazing display of centripetal force. Once you get started, it's almost habit forming. Left untreated, you'll be spinning everything in sight!

Here's What You'll Need

- Clear latex balloon (9-inch helium balloons from a party store work great)
- Penny

Let's Try It!

1. Squeeze a penny through the mouth of a clear balloon. Make sure that the penny goes all the way into the balloon so that there is no danger of it being sucked out while you are blowing up the balloon.

2. Blow up the balloon. When properly inflated, the balloon will be almost clear in the middle and cloudy at area near the neck and at the end opposite the neck.

Note: The cloudiness at the ends is unstretched latex. If the balloon is completely clear, all over, it is over inflated.

3. Tie off the balloon and you're ready to go.

4. Grip the balloon at the stem end as you would a bowling ball. The neck of the balloon will be

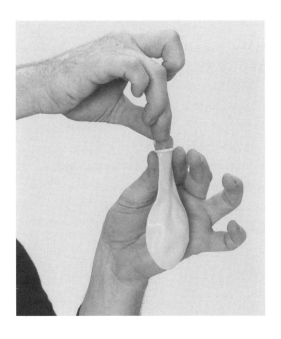

in your palm and your fingers and thumb will extend down the sides of the balloon.

5.   While holding the balloon palm down, swirl it in a circular motion. The penny may bounce around at first, but it will soon begin to roll around the inside of the balloon. The best orbit or path for the coin is one parallel to the floor.

6.   Once the coin begins spinning, use your other hand to stabilize the balloon. The penny should continue to spin for 30 seconds or so.

Take It Further

Try using different sized coins and comparing your record times. Does the size of the coin make any difference?

Ok, What's Going On Here?

The "Spinning Penny" is almost like science poetry in motion. To understand how and why it works, you have to look at the forces that are acting on the penny. The shape of the balloon makes the penny move in a circular path—otherwise the penny would want to continue to move in a straight line. Another force to consider is friction. There's very little friction between the edge of the penny and the balloon which would cause the penny to slow down and stop.

The penny in this balloon is a good example of what scientists call a *gyroscope*. Another example is a common toy top. Just as a spinning "top" resists tipping over while it's spinning, so does the penny. The gyroscopic action of the penny provides stability to its orbit within the balloon. Compare the behavior of a gyroscope to that of the penny spinning in the balloon. A gyroscope is essentially a spinning mass, and so is the penny. Once the disk (mass) of the gyroscope starts spinning, it resists tipping on its axis of rotation.

Inertia is the tendency of an object to stay in motion until a force acts upon it. The inertia of the penny keeps the it moving inside the balloon, but the force of gravity is what eventually causes the penny to stop moving.

You might have heard someone use the term *centrifugal force* when explaining the science of things that go around in a circle. Here's a great science secret … centrifugal force does not exist. That's right, centrifugal force is a *pseudo* or "false" force. When we spin around in a circle, it feels like we're being pulled away from the center. "Centrifugal" is Latin for center-fleeing, and that's what we feel, but the real force in action here is called *centripetal force,* or the center-seeking force. This is a force that is always directed *toward* the center of the circle and is actually responsible for keeping the penny moving in a circular motion inside the balloon.

To really understand the concept of centripetal force, you will need a much deeper understanding of Newton's First Law of Motion and some good math skills to work out the equations. Let's hope that the "Spinning Penny" experiment inspires you to sign up for a physics class in high school. Amaze the teacher with your cool experiment and she'll amaze you with an even better understanding of the Laws of Motion.

> **NEWTON'S FIRST LAW OF MOTION:**
>
> An object at rest tends to stay at rest and an object in motion tends to stay in motion with the same speed and in the same direction unless acted upon by an unbalanced force.

Screaming Balloon

You've tried spinning a penny, now take it one giant leap forward You won't believe what happens when you use a hex nut. Be sure to buy enough supplies for all of your friends because there's nothing better than a room filled with screaming balloons. Oh, it's also a great way to learn about the science of sound.

Here's What You'll Need

- Clear latex balloon (9-inch helium balloons from a party store work great)
- Some 1/4" hex nuts from the local hardware store

Let's Try It!

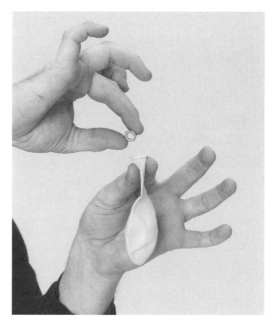

1. Squeeze the hex nut through the mouth of the balloon. Make sure that the hex nut goes all the way into the balloon so that there is no danger of it being sucked out while blowing up the balloon.
2. Blow up the balloon, but be careful not to over-inflate the balloon as it will easily burst. Tie off the balloon and you're ready to go.
3. Grip the balloon at the stem end as you would a bowling ball. The neck of the balloon will be in your palm and your fingers and thumb will extend down the sides of the balloon.
4. While holding the balloon, palm down, swirl it in a circular motion. The hex nut may bounce around at first, but it will soon begin to roll around the inside of the balloon. What is that sound? Could the balloon be screaming?
5. Once the hex nut begins to spin, use your other hand to stabilize

the balloon. Your hex nut should continue to spin for 10 seconds or more.

Take It Further

What happens when you change the size of the balloon or the size of the hex nut? In the previous experiment, why didn't the spinning penny make a similar noise? Try using a marble in place of a hex nut. Does the marble make the balloon "scream?"

Experiment with different sizes of hex nuts or any other circular object whose edges might vibrate against the balloon and create a strange screaming-like sound.

Ok, What's Going On Here?

This is actually a 2 for 1 experiment—you're learning about the science of motion and sound. The hex nut circles inside the balloon due to *centripetal* force (see the "Spinning Penny" experiment).

What makes this experiment different from the previous one with the spinning penny is the shape of the hex nut. A hex nut has six sides, and these flat edges cause the hex nut to bounce or vibrate inside the balloon. The screaming sound is made by the sides of the hex nut vibrating against the inside wall of the balloon.

Naked Eggs

This answers the age-old question . . . . Which came first, the rubber egg or the rubber chicken? It's easy to make a rubber or "naked" egg if you understand the chemistry of removing the hard eggshell. What you're left with is a totally embarrassed naked egg and a cool piece of science.

Here's What You'll Need

- Raw egg
- Tall glass
- Vinegar
- *Patience* (this one takes a little while)

Let's Try It!

1. Place the egg in a tall glass or jar and cover the egg with vinegar. Look closely at the egg. Do you see any bubbles forming on the shell?

2. Leave the egg in the vinegar for a full 24 hours.

3. It's time to change the vinegar on the second day. Carefully pour the old vinegar down the drain and cover the egg with fresh vinegar. Place the glass with the vinegar and egg in a safe place for a week—that's right—7 days! Don't disturb the egg but pay close attention to the bubbles forming on the surface of the shell (or what's left of it).

4. One week later, pour off the vinegar and carefully rinse the egg with water. The egg looks translucent because the outside shell is gone! The only thing that remains is the delicate membrane of the egg. You've successfully made an egg without a shell. Okay, you didn't really make the egg—chicken made the egg—and you just stripped away the chemical that gives the egg its strength.

into its calcium and carbonate parts (in simplest terms). The calcium part floats around in the solution while the carbonate part reacts to form the carbon dioxide bubbles that you see.

Some of the vinegar will also sneak through, or *permeate*, the egg's membrane and cause the egg to get a little bigger. That's why the egg is even more delicate if you handle it. If you shake the egg, you can see the yolk sloshing around in the egg white. Yes, you've made a pickled egg. But be careful. If the membrane breaks, the egg's insides will spill out into the vinegar.

Take It Further

Do organic or free-range eggs have an eggshell that is stronger or weaker than generic eggs? Conduct your own test on several different kinds of eggs all at the same time to observe any differences in the time required for the vinegar to dissolve the shell.

Ok, What's Going On Here?

Let's start with the bubbles you saw forming on the shell. The bubbles are carbon dioxide gas. Vinegar is an acid called acetic acid and white vinegar from the grocery store is usually about 5% vinegar and 95% water. Egg shells are made up of calcium carbonate. The vinegar reacts with the calcium carbonate by breaking the chemical

Soap Soufflé

Ivory Soap … it's the soap that floats. But why? Discover the secret behind this floating sensation by cooking the whole bar of soap in the microwave. That's right, the microwave oven! You won't believe your eyes!

Here's What You'll Need

- Bar of Ivory soap
- Various bars of other brands of soap
- Deep bowl of water (or a plastic tub)
- Paper towel
- Microwave oven
- An adult assistant

Let's Try It!

1. Fill the bowl with water.

2. Drop the bars of soap in the bowl of water. Notice how all of the bars of soap sink except for the Ivory brand soap. Why?

3. Remove the Ivory soap from the water and break it in half to see if there are any pockets of air hiding in the middle of the bar.

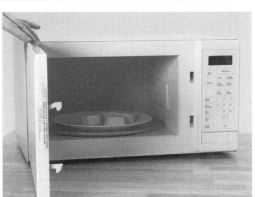

If there are, that would make the soap float, right? But there are no pockets of air, are there? So it must be some other property of the soap.

4. Place the bar of Ivory soap in the middle of a piece of paper towel and place the whole thing in the center of the microwave oven.

Note: This experiment requires adult supervision and permission to use the microwave oven.

5. Cook the bar of soap on HIGH for 2 minutes. Don't take your eyes off the bar of soap as it begins to expand and erupt into beautiful puffy clouds. Be careful not to overcook your soap soufflé.

6. Allow the soap to cool for a minute or so before touching it. Amazing... it's puffy but rigid. Don't waste the soap... take it into the shower or bath. It's still great soap with a slightly different shape and size.

Take It Further

Try the same experiment on any bar of soap other than Ivory. Do you see the same results? If you have an older bar of Ivory soap around the house, do a side-by-side comparison test between the older soap and a brand new bar from the store. Does the age of the soap have any affect on the size of the soap soufflé?

Ok, What's Going On Here?

Ivory soap is one of the few brands of bar soap that floats in water. But when you broke the bar of soap into several pieces, there were no large pockets of air. If it floats in water, and has no pockets of air, it must mean that the soap itself is less dense than water. Ivory soap floats because it has air pumped into it during the manufacturing process.

The air-filled soap was actually discovered by accident in 1890 by an employee at Proctor and Gamble. While mixing up a batch of soap, the employee forgot to turn off his mixing machine before taking his lunch break. This caused so much air to be whipped into the soap that the bars floated in water. The response by the public was so favorable that Proctor and Gamble continued to whip air into the soap and capitalized on the mistake by marketing their new creation as "The Soap that Floats!"

Why does the soap expand in the microwave? This is actually very similar to what happens when popcorn pops. Here's the secret: Inside of those air bubbles, there is water. There is also

water caught up in the matrix of the soap itself. The expanding effect is caused when the water that is inside the soap is heated. The water vaporizes, forming bubbles, and the heat also causes trapped air to expand. Likewise, the heat causes the soap itself to soften and become pliable.

This effect is actually a demonstration of "Charles' Law." Charles' Law states that as the temperature of a gas increases, so does its volume. When the soap is heated, the molecules of air in the soap move quickly, causing them to move far away from each other. This causes the soap to puff up and expand to an enormous size. Other brands of soap without whipped air tend to heat up and melt in the microwave.

Eating Nails for Breakfast

Have you ever taken the time to read the nutritional information on your box of breakfast cereal? You'll find that your cereal contains more than just wheat and corn. In fact, you'll notice that your cereal contains sodium, potassium, calcium, and iron. . . . Iron? Some nails are made from iron! Could you be eating nails for breakfast? Well, not really, but certain cereals do have a very high iron content. To better explain this, try the following experiment.

Here's What You'll Need

- Box of iron-fortified breakfast cereal (Total works best)
- Measuring cup
- Super strong magnet

Note: Magnets come in all shapes and sizes and different strengths. Regular household magnets won't work as well for this experiment or the next one. Ask a sales person at your local hardware store to help you find a strong magnet for a science experiment. The strongest magnets in the world are called Neodymium *magnets or "rare-earth" magnets. They are 10 times stronger than standard ceramic magnets and are commonly used in speakers and computer disc drives. It is possible to pull the iron out of the money using a standard magnet, but you'll get much better results using a Neodymium magnet.*

- Plastic dinner plate
- Resealable plastic bag (quart size works great)

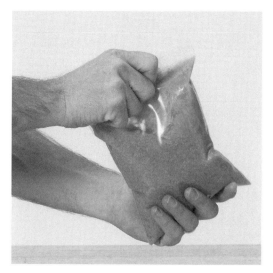

Let's Try It!

1. Open the box of cereal and pour a small pile of flakes on the plate. Crush them into tiny pieces with your fingers. Spread out the pile so it forms a single layer of crumbs on the plate.

Bring the magnet close to the layer of crumbs (but don't touch any) and see if you can get any of the pieces to move. Take your time. If you get a piece to move slightly without touching it, that piece may contain some metallic iron.

2. Firmly press the magnet directly onto the crumbs but don't move it. Lift it up and look underneath to see if anything is clinging to the magnet. Several little pieces may be stuck there. Is it the magnet being attracted to static electricity, or just sticky cereal? It could be the iron! Throw away the small pile of cereal and clean off your

magnet in order to move onto the next step.

3. Pour water into the plate and float a few flakes on the surface. Hold the magnet close to (but not touching) a flake, and see if the flake moves across the water toward the magnet. (The movement may be very slight, so be patient.) With practice, you can pull the flakes across the water, spin them, and even link them together in a chain. Hmmm. . . . There must be something that's responding to the magnet. Could it be metallic iron? In your cereal?!

4. It's time to mix up a batch of cereal soup to further investigate the claims of iron in your breakfast cereal. Open a quart size zipper lock bag and measure one cup of cereal (that's equal to one serving according to the information on the side of the cereal box) into the empty bag. Fill the bag half full with water and carefully seal it, leaving an air pocket inside.

5. Mix the cereal and the water by squeezing and smooshing the bag until the contents become a brown, soupy mixture. This may take a long time. In fact, you may want to let it sit for an hour or so until the cereal softens completely.

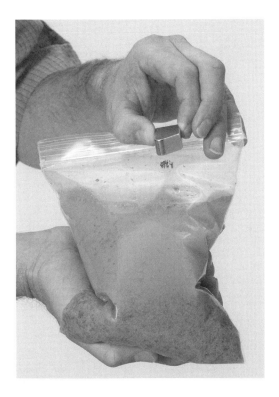

Note: Warm water will speed up the process.

6. Make sure the bag is tightly sealed and lay it on a flat side in the palm of your hand. Place the strong magnet on top of the bag. Put your other hand on top of the magnet and flip the whole thing over so the magnet is underneath the bag. Slowly slosh the contents of the bag in a circular motion for 15 or 20 seconds. The idea is to attract any free moving bits of metallic iron in the cereal to the magnet.

7. Use both hands again and flip the bag and magnet over so the magnet is on top. Gently squeeze the bag to lift the magnet a little

above the cereal soup. Don't move the magnet just yet. Look closely at the edges of the magnet where it's touching the bag. You should be able to see tiny black specks on the inside of the bag around the edges of the magnet. That's the iron!

8. Keep one end of the magnet touching the bag and draw little circles. As you do, the iron will gather into a bigger clump and be much easier to see. Few people have ever noticed iron in their food, so you can really impress your friends with this one. When you're finished, simply pour the soup down the drain and rinse the bag.

Take It Further

By this time, your brain should be overflowing with questions? Why is there iron in your cereal? Take a trip to the grocery store to investigate the contents of other cereals. What other brands claim to have iron? Conduct the same experiment using other brands of cereal

to see if you can find more magnetic black stuff. Could it really be iron?

Ok, What's Going On Here?

Many breakfast cereals are fortified with food-grade iron (chemical symbol: Fe) as a mineral supplement. Metallic iron is digested in the stomach and eventually absorbed in the small intestine. If all of the iron from your body were extracted, you'd have enough iron to make two small nails.

Iron is found in a very important component of blood called hemoglobin. Hemoglobin is the compound in red blood cells that carries oxygen from the lungs so it can be utilized by the body. *It's iron in the hemoglobin that gives blood its red appearance.*

A diet without enough iron can cause you to be tired, catch diseases easier, and make your heart and breathing rates too fast. Food scientists say that a healthy adult requires about 18 mg of iron each day. As you can see, iron plays a very important part in maintaining a healthy body. Eat up!

Money in a Blender—A Money Smoothie

It's true . . . money is magnetic! So, the only logical question that follows is, "Can you get the iron out of a dollar bill?" You'll be amazed at how much iron is in a single dollar bill. You'll need to get your hands on a dollar bill and a strong magnet to uncover an amazing secret.

Here's What You'll Need

- $1 bill (be sure to borrow it from a friend)
- Kitchen blender
- Water
- Quart-sized zipper-lock bag
- Strong magnet (see note in "Eating Nails for Breakfast" experiment)
- An adult assistant

Let's Try It!

1. You'll need a dollar bill. Now you could just dig down deep into your own pocket to find a bill or you can take Bob Becker's advice and borrow the bill from a friend. Hey, why should you have to provide the entertainment and pay for it too? Hold the neodymium magnet near the bottom of the bill.

Notice how the bill is attracted to the magnet.

2. Fill the blender half full with water (between 3 and 4 cups).

3. After the bill has been thoroughly examined to verify that it's real, drop the dollar bill into the blender and put on the lid.

4. What's next? Make dollar bill soup! Grind it, blend it, liquefy it . . . just make sure it's torn into thousands of little pieces.

5. After the blender has been grinding away for about a minute, stop it and pour the contents into the resealable plastic bag.

6. Place the neodymium magnet in the palm of your hand and place the bag of money soup on top of the magnet. Place your last remaining hand on top of the bag and rock the slurry back and forth in an effort to draw all of the iron to the magnet. Flip the bag over and look closely at the iron that is attracted to the magnet. You can slowly pull the magnet away from the bag to reveal the iron!

Take It Further

It's easy to suggest repeating the experiment with a $5 or a $10, but don't waste your money. Hey, this experiment already cost you a buck and you don't even know the secret. Keep reading.

Ok, What's Going On Here?

The secret is very simple… The government uses specially made

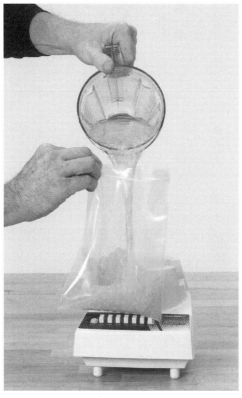

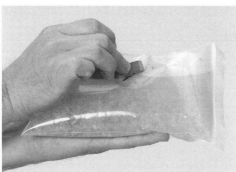

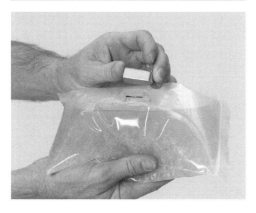

magnetic inks to print money. This makes it easy for vending machines to "read" the dollar bills, for example, and to determine if the money is real or counterfeit. The blender does a great job of tearing up the paper and releasing the magnetic ink into the water. Of course, metallic iron does not dissolve in water, but instead float around waiting for a magnet to pull it away from the fibers of the paper.

Here's a helpful tip... Make sure that you really shred the money in the blender for a few minutes to rip apart the paper and release the ink. When you turn off the blender, pour the blended money into zipper-lock bag right away – don't allow the money (and the iron) to settle to the bottom of the blender.

Here's something that's interesting... Is it illegal to destroy a dollar bill? According to U.S. Title 18, Chapter 17, Section 331, it's legal. This section of the law prohibits among other things, fraudulent alteration and mutilation of coins and paper money. This statue does not, however, prohibit the mutilation of currency if it's done without fraudulent intent. In other words, it's legal as long as you do not try to put the money back into circulation. So, don't spend all of your free time trying to glue the ground up dollar bill back together and then try to buy a candy bar with the money. Bottom line... don't try to spend the blended money and you won't have to spend any of your free time in jail.

The Tablecloth Trick

The classic whip-off the tablecloth trick is a must for any aspiring science demonstrator who wants to be amazing! It's guaranteed to either bring down the house or to get you into a lot of hot water. The idea is really quite simple: yank the tablecloth out from under a beautiful place setting without destroying the meal. It's easy if you take a science lesson from Sir Isaac Newton.

Here's What You'll Need

- Tablecloth

Note: The secret to your success is to make a tablecloth without any hems. For practice purposes, cut a piece of cloth that is approximately 3 foot square. You can graduate to a larger size as you perfect your skill.

- A tabletop that is perfectly flat, preferably with a straight edge.
- Dinner plates, saucers, and glasses—the heavier the better. Look carefully at the bottoms to make sure that the bottom surface is smooth.

Let's Try It!

1. Spread the tablecloth out onto the tabletop with about two feet of the tablecloth on the table. Place the cups, plates, and utensils on top of the tablecloth close to the edge of the cloth (for starters).

2. The trick is to grab the ends of the tablecloth with both hands and quickly pull the cloth down and away from the table. The key is the quick, downward motion— almost like you're whipping or yanking the cloth away. Keep saying to yourself, "Pull down . . . not out." Make sure to pull straight too, and not at an angle to the table.

3. The only way to make this work is to just do it! If you're nervous, start with only a dinner plate and do it over a carpeted floor. You'll be amazed when it works, and you'll add a saucer, then a cup,

and so on. Okay, stop reading this and try it!

Take It Further

Experimentation with Mom's best dinnerware will get you into big trouble. In this case, "taking it further" might get you into a world of trouble. Instead of testing out different plates, bowls and glasses, try experimenting with different masses on the plates. Make the plate or bowl heavier by adding a piece of fruit or something with some weight. Is it easier or harder to whip off the tablecloth?

Ok, What's Going On Here?

After you take your bows and graciously accept your standing ovation, be sure to thank Sir Isaac Newton for his help in making you an overnight success. Plain and simple, the secret is *inertia*. Newton first described inertia as the tendency for an object at rest to remain at rest until a force acts upon the object.

In terms of the tablecloth trick, inertia is important because according to the law, the objects (the stuff on the table) will not move unless an outside force moves them. This is known as Newton's First Law of Motion.

There are three different parts of this experiment to discuss. Initially, all of the objects (the plate, bowl, cup, utensils) are at rest (not moving). According to Netwon's First Law, objects at rest tend to stay at rest. When you pull the cloth, friction acts on the objects in the direction of the pull for a short time. The tablecloth is slippery, so these forces are small and the cloth sneaks out from underneath the objects. If you do it just right, everyone will be amazed. If you don't do it right, you're busted. Good luck talking your way out of this one.

The Egg Drop

Get ready for some fun! The goal is to get the egg into the glass of water but there are a few obstacles—a pie pan and the fact that the egg is perched high atop a cardboard tube. Sir Isaac Newton might have to come to the rescue of this amazing table trick.

Here's What You'll Need

- Small ball to practice with, if desired
- Cardboard tube
- Pie pan
- Raw eggs
- Water
- Large drinking glass
- Oh, you might need a few paper towels to clean up your practice mess!

Let's Try It!

1. Fill the large drinking glass about three-quarters full with water and center the pie pan on top of the glass. Place the cardboard tube on the plate, positioning it directly over the water. Carefully set the egg (or practice ball) on top of the cardboard tube.

2. With your writing hand, smack the edge of the dinner plate horizontally. Make sure you follow through. (Tennis, anyone?) It's important that you use a pretty solid hit, so plan on chasing the plate and tube.

3. Your astonished friends will watch the egg plop nicely into

the water. It's even more fun to watch someone else try to drop the egg. Science is so cool!

Take It Further

You could test longer tubes, more or less water, different liquids in the glass, different water containers, and heavier or lighter falling objects. So much science and so much fun!

Ok, What's Going On Here?

Credit for this one has to go to Sir Isaac Newton and his First Law of Motion. He said that since the egg is not moving while it sits on top of the tube, that's what it wants to do: not move. You applied enough force to the plate to cause it to zip out from under the cardboard tube (there's not much friction against the container). The edge of the pie pan hooked the bottom of the tube, which then sailed off with the plate. Basically, you knocked the support out from under the egg. For a brief nanosecond or two, the egg didn't move because it was already stationary (not moving). But then, as usual, the force of gravity took over and pulled the egg straight down toward the center of the Earth. Also according to Mr. Newton's First Law, once the egg was moving, it didn't want to stop. The container of water interrupted the egg's fall, providing a safe place for the egg to stop moving so you could recover it unbroken. The gravity-pushed egg caused the water to splash out. Did someone get wet?

Flying Potatoes & Exploding Soda

The Secret to Creating Unforgettable Learning Experiences

 I've worked in television for many years, not as the evening anchor or the sports guy or even the weatherman. When the little red light comes on, it's my job to teach viewers how to do something amazing using ordinary stuff found around the house. What amazing things, you ask? Oh, things like how to make a high-powered potato launcher out of pencils and straws or how to make a 2-liter bottle of soda erupt into a 12-foot high fountain of fun.

That's right… you guessed it… when the red light comes on, I become the science guy – a modern day **Mr. Wizard,** so to speak.

But my first job was not in television. Fresh out of college with a teaching certificate in hand, I found a job in an elementary school teaching science. It didn't take long for me to discover that my style of teaching was somewhat different from my colleagues, who spent most of their time running off worksheets in the copy room. My kids laughed a lot (almost too much at times) and this soon caught the attention of neighboring teachers and their kids who were more than just a little curious. One colleague asked, "How can your students be learning when they're laughing so much?" Hmmm… I wonder if laughter and learning go hand in hand? The answer is, yes!

I have to attribute most of my success as a teacher to my first class of 3rd graders. Over the course of nine months, they taught me the importance of using humor to create experiences that transcended the four walls of the classroom and somehow made it to the dinner table as a topic of conversation.

"What did you do in school today?"

"Not much. Oh… I remember something… Mr. Spangler made us get into a big circle and hold hands… then he shocked us with 50,000 volts to teach us about electricity."

I got lots of calls from parents that first year of teaching, and it didn't take long for word to spread that things were a little different in the new teacher's class.

One of those parents just happened to work for the local NBC television affiliate in Denver. She invited me down to the station one day after school and asked if I would bring along a few science experiments from my class... including that shocking machine. In no time, I had a group of television executives making slime, shooting potatoes and holding hands in a big circle while I delivered the shock. That one command performance opened the door for me into a much bigger classroom. I went from 23 kids to over a million viewers each week as the host of a nationally syndicated children's program called *News for Kids.*

My executive producer spelled out my mission in the clearest terms possible. "Your job is not to teach science. Your job is to grab the viewer's attention and show them that learning is fun. Make them laugh and the learning will follow." These marching orders soon became my mantra and the advice that I give to parents and teachers today.

3-2-1 Blast Off!

As part of a promotional tour for the television show, I found myself on the road visiting children in schools across the country with my bag of cool gadgets and science demonstrations. Let's just say that there's nothing terribly glamorous about doing school assemblies. The best-case scenario is that a bunch of kids are crammed into the cafeteria and forced to sit on the floor, while the guest speaker is forced to shout because the P.E. teacher is using the microphone as a doorstop. On this particular occasion, the setting was an elementary school in the heart of Salt Lake City. Nearly 700 children squeezed their way into the cafeteria and the principal's introduction was nothing short of inspirational.

"Hey kids... listen up. There's a guy here who wants to show you something and I want you to be good for a change. If I catch anyone throwing stuff at the speaker like you did last time, I'm shutting this circus down. [Turning to me] Okay... they're all yours."

With an introduction like that, things could only get better. Up to this point, I had never really taught kindergartners, but I soon learned that these little people have a tendency to grab parts of your body as a sign of affection! I did most of the show with a five year old latched onto my leg. Thankfully, the kids liked the demos and I survived my first of two presentations. As the sea of children started to file out of the room, I noticed that one of the kindergartners was not ready to leave. In fact, he wanted to talk to me. As he approached, I could tell that he was a little nervous. He pulled at his pant leg and squirmed as if it might be time to find a bathroom. As I kneeled down, he began to talk.

"Ummm… hey guy. Guess what?"

"What?"

"I like rockets."

"Me, too!"

"And you know what else? I know how to make a rocket… and some day I will make a rocket that can fly to the sun!"

Well, here's a tough fork in the road. I can't tell him *no* because I would crush his dream, and I can't say *great* because I would be lying. They just don't teach you this stuff in college! I looked him right in the eyes, and with compassion in my voice I said, "I like your idea… but if your rocket gets too close to the sun, it will melt."

He looked at me only the way a kindergartner could and said, "I'm doing it at night, duh!" It was as if I had swallowed the bait and he was reeling in the catch of the day. The best part is that I had heard someone tell me the same joke years before, but I had never heard it told by a kindergartner! Then the light bulb in my head went on. Behind every funny kindergartner there's a funnier person called a teacher. I immediately looked over the sea of kids to find his kindergarten teacher looking right at me with a huge grin as she mouthed the phrase, "Gotcha!" I turned my attention back to the little comedian and said, "You are so funny!" His reply was phrased with a sense of apprehension, "I don't know why everyone thinks that joke is so funny."

What? Didn't the kid get it? Then it hit me like a ton of bricks. This little boy still believed. In his way of thinking, all things are possible. What was so funny to me and to his teacher, offered little in the way of humor to him because his world was filled with limitless possibilities. What a concept! His teacher and I shared a laugh, a hug and the promise that we would never lose our child-like joy of learning.

That's So Dumb!

After almost eight years of teaching, I thought that I had a pretty good handle on what makes kids tick. Then my wife blessed me with our first child. His name is Jack and he's filled with a genuine sense of wonder. Occasionally, I get the honor and privilege of being the "helping dad" at Jack's preschool. I don't know how much "helping" goes on when I'm at school because I find myself playing with the best of them. It doesn't take long to forget my writing deadlines or lesson plans because I'm so caught up in the art of playing.

Oh, yes… there is an art and science to playing. One day, I zoomed in on the building blocks where I found a little guy who was having problems keeping his structure from falling down. It was helping dad to the rescue! I made a recommendation to my playing partner that we use big blocks on the bottom of the tower to make it more stable and to keep it from falling. Then we could build upon this solid foundation to create a building taller than anything the preschool had ever seen. He stopped me in mid-sentence, looked at me with those 4-year-old eyes and said, "That's so dumb! It's supposed to fall over." What was I thinking?

What else did I learn? Toy cars can fly. Red paint is boring, but red and green paint mix together is cool. It's more fun to color outside the lines and leave the inside white. It fun to paint your hand. And it's really fun to misname everything! Call the fish a hamster or the bird a flying alligator and you hit a nerve. Soon I found myself dressing a T-Rex in Barbie clothes and calling it Diana Sawyer. I was learning the art of 4-year-old playtime.

As teachers and parents, we must remember that playing and learning go hand in hand. It took a simple experience like this to remind me that I didn't need to have a structured activity or worksheet to make a discovery, to explore something new, or just to have fun. I needed this experience to remind me that I must MAKE the time to laugh and play so that I can continue to learn and grow as a parent and a teacher.

Okay, That's Funny

Yes, this would be the perfect opportunity for the "science guy" to launch into a discussion about the science of humor—to quote amazing statistics and to expound upon the volumes of brain research revealing the incredible psychological and physiological ramifications of humor. NOT! Let's face it, if I were that smart, I would not be blowing stuff up on morning television as a means of entertaining the masses as they drink their first cup of coffee. I guess I don't need statistics or high-level research to convince me that humor is one of the most effective tools we can use to create unforgettable learning experiences.

If you are an adult reading this book and you try only one activity, you must do the Mentos Geyser (see page 20) Round up the materials—Mentos mint candies and a bottle of your favorite diet soda (I use Diet Coke). Gather a group of friends, co-workers, kids or just a bunch of people you don't know around the bottle of soda. Remove all of the Mentos candies from the wrapper as you explain to your friends that you have discovered how to make a new flavor of soda. Twist off the soda cap. The goal is for you to drop all of the Mentos into the bottle of soda at the same time. The method that works best for me is to use a piece of scrap paper to form a tube to hold the stack of Mentos. Fill the tube with the candies keeping your finger covering the bottom of the tube so the Mentos don't fall out. Ask everyone to move in close to the bottle. Position the paper tube holding the stack of mints directly over the opening of the bottle. When you're ready, let all of the Mentos fall into the diet soda. Oh, I forgot to mention this minor detail… run!

There's just something humorous about watching a group of people run for their lives as an 18-foot tall stream of soda erupts from the bottle. Mentos are a unique candy that has tiny pits all over the surface. The dissolved carbon dioxide gas in the soda run to the pits which causes the incredible eruption of gas. If chemistry class had been this much fun, you might have slept less and learn more. Just give it a try and I promise you'll never look at a roll of Mentos candy the same way.

You just learned the final science secret in this book…

Secrets # 250, 251, 252, 253...

Keep Track of Your Own Science Discoveries!!
(Especially the Ones Your Teacher Doesn't Know About)

Real scientists write things down so they can share them with others and test their assumptions. Here's your chance to show what you can think up. Use the lines in the remaining pages of this book to keep track of your own insights, thoughts, discoveries, and hypotheses. Good luck!!

_____

_____

_____

_____

_____

_____

_____

_____

_____

_____

_____

_____

_____

_____

_____

_____

_____

_____

_____

About the Author

He's been described as the guy who shoots potatoes, makes toilet paper fly, and mixes up a perfect batch of slime. But his new title of the *Mentos Guy* might nudge out all of the others because of the recent popularity of his science experiments using the mint candy Mentos. If you're linked to the outside world via the internet, you just might have watched one of the erupting Mentos videos. He's just the guy who helped turn the Mentos Experiment into a pop culture phenomenon.

Steve Spangler is nationally known as a teacher's teacher who shares his passion for learning in the classroom, on the platform, and through the airwaves. Over the last ten years, Steve has made over 275 network television appearances as an authority on hands-on science. His eye-catching science demonstrations and kid-focused activities earned him an Emmy as the science host of NBC television's *News for Kids* in 1997. Steve continues to use the airwaves as his classroom to reach over a million viewers each week as the "science guy" on 9NEWS - KUSA-TV in Denver and online at **www.9news.com/spangler**.

Steve serves as the Director of the *National Hands-on Science Institute* in Denver where he coordinates the staff development training for 1,500 teachers nationwide.

With twelve years experience in the classroom, Steve continues to share his creative learning strategies and inquiry research as a consultant for the Littleton Public Schools in Colorado. The focus of his work centers around hands-on learning and student motivation.

When faced with having to make a career decision, Steve combined his experiences as a teacher and a toy designer to start his own business dedicated to creating products that make learning science fun. As the founder and CEO of *Be Amazing! Toys*, Steve and his creative team of designers developed more than 50 educational toys and science related products for companies like *Scholastic*, the *Discovery Channel*, and *Toys R' Us*.

What is Steve doing right now? He's probably making some gadget ooze, bubble, fizz, bounce, smoke, or maybe he's creating a new idea to get another human being turned on to life's small wonders.

To learn more science secrets, visit **www.SteveSpanglerScience.com**.